FORMATION TO FOUNDATION

A STARTUP GUIDE TO CORPORATE STRATEGY

W. M. CORNELL

TAWCarlisle Publishing

Copyright

Table of Contents

1

WHY STRUCTURE MATTERS

"Your business structure isn't just paperwork — it's your foundation. And just like you wouldn't build a house on sand, you can't build a scalable company on shaky structure."

— W.M. Cornell

Starting Where You Are

Let me tell you something from experience — most of us start this journey not with a perfectly mapped-out business plan, but with a little grit, a lot of heart, and a vision we can't shake. That's beautiful. And terrifying. And exactly right.

Some of the greatest empires — Amazon, Apple, Spanx — didn't begin with perfect structure. They began with ideas so compelling that the founders couldn't not pursue them. But what took those companies from garage concepts to global corporations wasn't just product-market fit — it was a *willingness to build structure around the chaos.*

"Every legacy business started as someone's blurry dream. Structure gave it shape."

1

But what transforms a good idea into a living, breathing enterprise isn't just hustle — it's architecture. Thoughtful, legal, financial, operational structure. It's about building something you can *trust to carry weight*, even when things get heavy. It's about knowing that your foundation is strong enough to support not just your vision — but your future employees, your clients, your partnerships, your reputation.

Let me share a brief moment from one of my earliest ventures. I had a contract, a logo, and even a few clients. But no formal entity. No operating agreement. I was invoicing from my personal checking account. One late payment and a contract dispute later, I found myself on the edge of losing it all — not just financially, but mentally. That was the wake-up call. I didn't just need a service to offer — I needed a structure to grow into.

You don't need to experience a crisis to create structure. That's what this guide is here for. To give you the wisdom *before* the storm. Because once you've weathered a few tough quarters, structure becomes your shelter, not just your paperwork.

And let's be honest — if you don't put structure in place, life will eventually demand it from you. The question is: will you build your foundation now, or patch the cracks later?

The best businesses don't just survive storms — they prepare for them in advance.

What Is Business Structure, Really?

Business structure is how your idea becomes *real*. It's the bridge between imagination and implementation.

Highly Searched Keywords: business structure for startups, best business structure for entrepreneurs, how to start a company legally, LLC vs sole proprietorship

It's how you:

- Protect your personal assets
- Qualify for funding and capital
- Establish boundaries and rights within your team
- Get serious in the eyes of clients, vendors, partners, and the IRS

Structure dictates how you:

- Pay yourself
- Pay others
- Protect yourself
- Plan your growth

Structure determines your ability to:

- Attract investors
- Form strategic partnerships
- Acquire business credit
- Navigate mergers or acquisitions
- Scale internationally

It determines how you pay taxes, who owns what, and what happens if someone sues you. But more than that, it signals to the world — and yourself — that this isn't just a side project anymore. It's a company.

Let's take the limited liability company (LLC) — created in Wyoming in 1977 and widely adopted in the 1990s. Before this innovation, small business owners either had to operate as sole proprietors (putting personal assets on the line) or incorporate (which was complicated and expensive). The LLC changed that. It created a safe middle ground: flexible, protective, and scalable.

In 1980, fewer than 5% of small businesses used an LLC structure. Today, over 70% of new small businesses do — because it strikes a critical balance: protection without unnecessary complexity. That's not just legal evolution — it's economic empowerment.

And beyond LLCs, understanding other options — from sole proprietorships to S-Corps and C-corps — gives you the clarity to not just build something, but build it the *right* way for your long-term vision. We'll unpack all of this in the next section.

> *"You don't need permission to get started — but you do need structure to stay in the game."*

Ask yourself: what type of business do I *want* to run five years from now? That answer should influence what structure you choose *today*.

The Emotion Behind the Paperwork

Highly Searched Keywords: how to register a business, small business startup checklist, business entity formation tips

I get it — paperwork feels boring. Forms, fees, state sites that look like they haven't been updated since 2002. But the emotion behind all of it? That's powerful.

Every time you file a form, you are:

- Naming your vision
- Claiming space in the market
- Accepting responsibility for how you'll show up

This isn't about bureaucracy. This is about identity. When you register your company, you're declaring: "I am here. I exist. I intend to contribute."

Think of it like this: your structure is the first contract you make with yourself. It's the moment when your inner entrepreneur shakes hands with your future CEO.

So don't look at structure as a chore. Look at it as a rite of passage. You're not just building a business. You're growing into a new level of stewardship.

Here's what happens after you register:

- You get your EIN (Employer Identification Number)
- You open a business bank account
- You create your operating agreement or bylaws

- You start separating your personal identity from your business identity — and that's powerful

"It's not just the name on the paperwork. It's the name on the legacy."

Grounding Yourself with the 5Ws

Highly Searched Keywords: how to define your target market, startup mission statement, how to identify your business niche

Before you form an LLC or choose a business name, you need to get quiet and clear. Let's revisit the classic five:

Who are you called to serve?

This is about audience, but it's also about alignment. Who do you resonate with? Who are you best positioned to help? Don't guess — investigate. Look at demographics, pain points, communities you understand deeply.

Exercise: Write down 3 different avatars (fictional customer profiles). What do they need? Where do they live? What keeps them up at night?

What solution do you provide?

Don't say "consulting" or "events" or "tech." Say, "I help nonprofits automate donor communications using AI-driven tools." Be crisp. Clear beats clever every time.

Pro Tip: If you can't explain your business in one sentence to a 10-year-old, go back to the drawing board.

When will you be ready to show up?

Some of you are reading this before launching. Others have been in business for a year but still don't feel official. Wherever you are, this question matters. Set a timeline. Honor it. Revise it when necessary — but never ignore it.

"A dream with no date is a wish. Set your start line."

Where will your impact be felt?

Online? Local community? A specific region? A particular niche of the internet? Your footprint matters — and determines your infrastructure needs.

Real-World Note: If you're serving clients on the East Coast but you live on the West, you need time zone strategy. If your audience lives on Instagram, your storefront better speak fluent visual storytelling.

Why should anyone trust *you* to solve this?

This is your differentiator. Your ethos. Your why. It's not always a resume answer — sometimes it's personal history, lived experience, deep empathy.

"Clarity doesn't come from movement. It comes from alignment."

Use the Visioning Worksheet in the Appendix to write these out. Revisit them often. These answers form your *anchor*, especially in times of uncertainty.

Gentle Reminders for New Founders

Keynotes: tips for first-time founders, how to start a business from scratch, new entrepreneur advice

- You don't have to know everything today. Just take the next step.
- You're allowed to ask for help — smart founders do it early.
- Done is better than perfect. Launch the beta, fix it live.
- You're not late. You're right on time — and right on purpose.
- Remember: courage is more important than credentials.
- There's no shame in starting small. There's danger in staying vague.
- Structure doesn't limit creativity. It protects it.
- Surround yourself with accountability — mentors, coaches, and advisors
- Treat your business like a business, even if it's still earning hobby money

This book isn't here to impress you. It's here to *walk with you*.

"Every founder is scared. The wise ones move anyway."

Let's lay that foundation. Not just in ink and filings — but in identity, clarity, and purpose.

2

CHOOSING THE RIGHT BUSINESS ENTITY

"Form follows function — and your business structure should always follow your long-term vision." — W.M. Cornell

Why This Decision Is More Than Just a Checkbox

Choosing your business entity is not just a bureaucratic necessity — it's a declaration of your company's identity and trajectory. In fact, for many entrepreneurs, this is the first strategic decision that lays the groundwork for legal compliance, tax efficiency, and investor readiness.

Let's be clear: the entity you choose affects how much you pay in taxes, how you're protected legally, how easy it is to raise money, and how scalable your business becomes.

Highly Searched Keywords: LLC vs S-Corp, best legal structure for startups, pros and cons of C-corporation, business entity for online business

It's not one-size-fits-all. So take this part seriously.

Entity Types Explained (With Heart)

1. Sole Proprietorship — *The Simplest Start*

This is the default for many solo entrepreneurs. If you've started selling a product or service and haven't registered anything officially, you're likely a sole proprietor.

- **Pros:**
    - Easiest and cheapest to form
    - Total control over decision-making
    - Simple tax filings (you file income on your personal tax return)
- **Cons:**
    - No legal separation between you and the business
    - You're personally liable for debts and lawsuits

"Sole proprietorships are like lemonade stands — great for testing, but risky to grow without structure."

2. Partnership — For When You Start with a Co-Founder

There are two main types: general partnerships and limited partnerships. Both are essentially agreements between two or more people to share ownership and responsibilities.

- **Pros:**
    - Shared workload and capital
    - Pass-through taxation (profits taxed once on owners' personal returns)
- **Cons:**
    - Partners are personally liable (unless it's a limited partnership)
    - Potential for disputes without a solid operating agreement

Founder's Tip: Draft an agreement upfront — even if it's your best friend. Especially if it's your best friend.

3. Limited Liability Company (LLC) — The Modern Standard for Small Businesses

This is one of the most popular structures for new entrepreneurs, and for good reason.

- **Pros:**
    - Protects your personal assets
    - Flexible tax options (you can be taxed as a sole proprietor, partnership, or even S-Corp)

11

- ○ Fewer corporate formalities than a C-Corp
- **Cons:**
  - ○ You may pay self-employment taxes on all profits
  - ○ Varies by state (some states have expensive fees and rules)

"If your business is your baby, the LLC is the crib — safety and support as you grow."

4. S-Corporation — For Tax-Savvy Owners Who Pay Themselves

An S-Corp isn't an entity type, but a tax election status you can choose (if you qualify).

- **Pros:**
  - ○ Avoids double taxation (income is passed to shareholders)
  - ○ You can pay yourself a salary and reduce self-employment taxes
- **Cons:**
  - ○ More paperwork and IRS scrutiny
  - ○ Shareholder limitations (e.g., must be U.S. citizens, max of 100 shareholders)

This is ideal for businesses generating steady income with few shareholders.

5. C-Corporation — Built for Scale and Investment

If you're planning to raise money, go public, or attract VCs, this is your structure.

- **Pros:**
  - No limit on shareholders
  - Investors prefer this format
  - Easier to offer employee stock options (ESOPs)
- **Cons:**
  - Double taxation (corporate profits and dividends)
  - Required board of directors, corporate minutes, and regular filings

"C-Corps are skyscrapers — not always the first build, but essential if you're aiming for the skyline."

Entity Comparison Chart

Type	Liability Protection	Taxation	Complexity	Ideal For
Sole Proprietorship	✕	Personal	Low	Testing an idea solo
Partnership	✕ (some ☑)	Personal	Medium	Two founders launching quickly
LLC	☑	Flexible	Medium	Service providers, small teams
S-Corp	☑	Pass-through	High	High-income solopreneurs
C-Corp	☑	Double tax	High	Venture-backed startups

How to Choose: 3 Strategic Filters

1. **Your Vision:**
   - Do you plan to stay lean, or grow big and fast?
   - Will you seek funding or stay bootstrapped?
2. **Your Risk Profile:**
   - Are you operating in a litigious industry?
   - Do you sell physical products or provide high-risk services?
3. **Your Money Flow:**
   - Will you be reinvesting most profits?
   - Are you building an asset or cash-flow lifestyle business?

"The right structure is the one that matches your future — not just your today."

Real Talk: What Most First-Time Founders Do

The vast majority of new entrepreneurs opt for an LLC, and many elect S-Corp status once revenue picks up. Why?

Because it offers:

- Flexibility
- Simplicity
- Legal protection
- Reasonable tax options

That said, if you're planning to raise venture capital, a Delaware C-Corp is still the gold standard.

Pro Insight: If you're unsure, start with an LLC. You can always convert it later with proper planning.

Step-by-Step: How to Form Your Entity

Highly Searched Keywords: how to file an LLC, best state to form LLC, how to start a business legally

1. Choose a business name (check your Secretary of State website)
2. File Articles of Incorporation (or Organization for an LLC)
3. Get an EIN from the IRS
4. Draft your operating agreement (LLC) or bylaws (corporation)
5. Open a business bank account
6. Register for any licenses or permits

Founder's Tip: Platforms like LegalZoom, Incfile, and ZenBusiness can streamline the process — but always read the fine print.

Final Thought: Structure Is Leadership

This isn't about choosing a form. It's about stepping into the role of a business owner. A CEO. A steward of something real.

When you choose a structure, you're not just filing papers. You're telling the world:

- "I take this seriously."
- "I'm protecting what I'm building."
- "I'm ready to grow."

"Paperwork doesn't make you legitimate. But doing it with purpose — that's the beginning of leadership."

3

BUILDING YOUR BRAND, VISION, AND OPERATING CULTURE — FROM THE INSIDE OUT

"Before your logo, before your launch, comes your legacy. Build that first." — W.M. Cornell

Brand Is Not a Logo — It's a Feeling

Branding is not just color palettes and fonts — it's how people experience your business. Your brand is the story people tell about you when you're not in the room. And in the startup phase, **you are the brand**.

Highly Searched Keywords: how to build a brand from scratch, branding for startups, brand voice and identity, startup branding tips

Whether you're creating a wellness company, a SaaS tool, or a luxury product — your brand should evoke emotion, create consistency, and build trust.

Start with these guiding questions:

- What 3 words do you want your business to be known for?
- If your business was a person, what would its personality be?
- What do you want people to feel after interacting with your product/service?

"Your brand is your handshake, your story, and your promise — all in one."

The Internal Foundation of a Brand:

1. **Vision Statement** — What future are you building?
2. **Mission Statement** — What are you doing now to reach that future?
3. **Core Values** — What principles guide how you behave and make decisions?

These three elements are your compass. Before you hire. Before you scale. Before you rebrand.

Your Vision Must Be Bigger Than Today

When you're just getting started, it's tempting to focus only on what's in front of you. But your vision should be expansive — something that guides and pulls you forward.

Visioning Exercise:

Write a page (yes, a full page) answering this:

- What does your business look like in 5 years?
- What does a day in your life look like when it's fully operational?
- What kind of impact have you made on your customers, your community, your family?

Use language that is emotional, sensory, and clear. This is not a pitch deck. This is for *you*. Keep it near. When doubt shows up — and it will — this is what you come back to.

"Your vision is not your vanity. It's your clarity."

The Five W's of Brand and Culture

Who do you serve?

- Not just demographics — but psychographics.
- What do they value? Fear? Aspire to?

What do you do differently?

- What transformation do you provide?
- How do you uniquely deliver your service?

When do people need you most?

- Is your offer seasonal, crisis-driven, or constant?
- What triggers your customer's journey?

Where do you operate?

- Physical? Virtual? Regional?
- Is your voice consistent across platforms?

Why do you exist?

- What problem are you solving?
- Why does your team care?

When these are clear, your brand becomes magnetic — it draws the right people and repels what's not aligned.

Culture Is What You Normalize

Culture is not a ping-pong table. It's the daily experience people have working with and for your brand.

Ask yourself:

- What gets celebrated here?
- What gets tolerated here?
- What gets ignored here?

Highly Searched Keywords: startup company culture, how to build company culture, core values for startups, employee engagement startup tips

Write a *Culture Code* (even if you're a team of one). Include:

- Communication norms
- Conflict resolution expectations
- Remote work policies
- Decision-making frameworks
- How you handle wins and losses

"If you don't define your culture, it will define itself — usually in ways you don't like."

Brand Identity vs. Brand Experience

- **Identity** is the visuals: logo, colors, fonts, etc.
- **Experience** is how people *feel* interacting with your company.

The most trusted brands obsess over consistency. It builds credibility.

Checklist to Review:

- Is your tone the same on social media and emails?
- Does your visual branding reflect your values?
- Are your website and onboarding materials easy to understand?
- Do your customers feel seen and supported after purchase?

Your Brand is Built Every Day

Not just in design meetings or mission statements — but in every:

- Email response
- Social media post
- Product delivery
- Team huddle
- Customer service reply

You are *always* branding.

> *"Whether you say it or not, your business is telling a story. Make sure it's the one you want remembered."*

4

LAYING OPERATIONAL GROUNDWORK — PROCESSES, SYSTEMS, AND THE POWER OF DOCUMENTATION

"Ideas make you a visionary. Systems make you a CEO." — W.M. Cornell

The Quiet Power of Systems

Startups often launch from pure passion — late nights, last-minute decisions, endless pivots. And while that fire is admirable, the real breakthrough happens when passion meets process. Systems turn inspiration into impact.

Highly Searched Keywords: business systems for startups, operational efficiency, how to build startup operations, small business automation, workflow optimization

Operations are the invisible scaffolding of your business. They enable consistency, reduce decision fatigue, and allow you to lead rather than chase fires. Your systems are your safety net — they catch your future before it collapses under pressure.

25

"If your business can't survive a sick day, it's not a business — it's a fragile hustle."

Consider Henry Ford's legendary assembly line. While the Model T changed transportation, it was Ford's operational breakthrough — the methodical, timed process of production — that revolutionized industry. Ford proved that innovation was not just about invention, but about delivery. Repeatable, scalable systems transform ideas into global movements.

Look at Starbucks: its coffee isn't what built its empire — its operations did. A barista in Tokyo can deliver the same order, experience, and output as one in Los Angeles. That's not magic — it's systemization.

"You don't rise to the level of your vision. You fall to the level of your systems." — James Clear

Founder's Journal Prompt: Systems Vision Exercise

- What areas of your business feel chaotic right now?
- If you had to step away for two weeks, what process would need to exist for your company to continue?
- Imagine onboarding a new team member. What do they need to know Day 1?

Take 15 minutes to free-write your answers. This reflection becomes the blueprint for your first systems manual.

What Are Operations?

Operations define the daily rhythm of your organization. They shape the experience of your clients, your team, and even your own stress levels. They answer:

- How do we deliver on our brand promise?
- What happens from the time someone discovers us to the time they refer us?
- How do we measure performance, optimize delivery, and recover from setbacks?

Operations include:

- Client onboarding
- Billing and invoicing
- Employee task management
- Inventory tracking
- Quality control
- Internal communication
- Crisis and error recovery protocols

"Operations are not the back-end. They are the backbone."

Too many founders confuse activity with progress. Operations give structure to creativity — not to stifle it, but to channel it. When you create a consistent operating rhythm, you free your mind for innovation.

Operations in History: A Lesson from the Apollo Program

NASA's moon landing wasn't just about astronauts — it was about operations. The Apollo Program involved over 400,000 people, coordinated across departments, vendors, engineers, and mission control. What made the mission successful wasn't just cutting-edge tech — it was an obsessive focus on checklists, communications protocols, and systems.

Their systems were so precise that even failure had a manual — and that operational brilliance saved lives during Apollo 13.

"In systems thinking, nothing is random — everything is orchestrated."

Common Operational Mistakes First-Time Founders Make (And How to Avoid Them)

1. **Over-Automating Too Early**
   Automate a mess and you just make it faster. First, refine your *manual* process. Then automate what works.
2. **Failing to Document**
   Your mind is not a filing cabinet. Document your systems so others can help, and so you don't become the bottleneck.
3. **Choosing Complicated Tools**
   Simple tools used consistently beat fancy ones used

sporadically. Use what makes sense, not what looks impressive.

4. **Ignoring Feedback Loops**
   Your team and your customers are constantly giving you operational insight — but are you listening? Make feedback a system.

"If your business runs on memory, urgency, and intuition — it's not sustainable. It's reaction, not operation."

Weekly Founder Ritual: The Operational Pulse Check

Schedule one hour each week to step *out* of the doing and into the designing. Ask:

- What worked well operationally this week?
- What broke? Why?
- What repetitive task should be documented or delegated?
- What decision caused delay — and could it be pre-decided?
- Did a team member or client run into friction? Can we remove it next time?

"The founder's calendar is a sacred blueprint. Make time to fix the future, not just survive today."

Build this habit and your operations will self-correct before crises emerge.

Sample Operating Checklist — "Client Onboarding SOP"

Stage 1: Pre-Onboarding

- ☑ Contract signed (via HelloSign)
- ☑ First invoice sent + paid
- ☑ Welcome email sent with next steps

Stage 2: Onboarding Call

- ☑ Schedule kick-off via Calendly
- ☑ Confirm tech/tool access
- ☑ Collect brand assets & docs

Stage 3: Setup + Launch

- ☑ Project management board created
- ☑ Task dependencies clarified
- ☑ Weekly touchpoints established

📥 *Download this checklist as a template in the Appendix.*

Real-World Quote from a Founder's Experience:

"When I first started my agency, I thought systems were for big companies. After I dropped a $5,000 client due to a simple missed email — I realized: systems are what make you look big before you are."
— Dana H., Founder of Emerge Agency

"Once I built a daily SOP, my stress cut in half. I finally stopped waking up at 3 a.m. thinking, 'Did I forget something?'"

BONUS SEGMENT: Operations by Business Type

- **E-commerce:** Fulfillment systems, returns protocols, inventory syncing
- **Service-Based:** Client CRM pipeline, invoicing, consultation scheduling
- **Nonprofit:** Donor database, volunteer onboarding, event workflows
- **SaaS Startups:** Product lifecycle management, user onboarding, ticketing

Identify your category and build your systems around recurring needs.

"The business model shapes the operational backbone."

5

FINANCIAL FUNDAMENTALS – BUDGETS, FORECASTS, AND KNOWING YOUR NUMBERS

"Revenue is vanity. Profit is sanity. Cash is reality." — Unknown

Money is more than numbers. It's the oxygen of your business — and if you run out, nothing else survives. Many first-time founders avoid the financials, hoping revenue alone will fix inefficiencies. But real leadership starts with clarity.

In this section, we'll build your financial literacy muscle. We'll go beyond the spreadsheets into the mindset of responsible stewardship — so you can make wise decisions, attract investors, and sleep well at night.

Highly searched keywords: startup budgeting template, cash flow vs profit, small business forecasting, how to set prices, startup financial projections, break-even analysis

The Three Financial Statements You Must Know

Let's break these down in simple language:

1. Profit & Loss Statement (P&L)

Think of this as your "report card" — it shows how much you earned and how much you spent in a specific period.

- Revenue – what you sold
- Expenses – what you paid to operate
- Net profit or loss – the difference

If you're in the red (negative net profit), don't panic — many businesses start there. What matters is understanding why and how to turn it around.

2. Balance Sheet

This is your "snapshot in time." It shows what your business owns and owes on a specific date.

- **Assets** — cash, equipment, inventory, accounts receivable
- **Liabilities** — loans, unpaid bills, credit lines
- **Equity** — what's left if you sold everything and paid off debts

Use your balance sheet to understand your solvency and short-term risk. It's also critical when applying for financing.

3. Cash Flow Statement

This tells the real story: how much money you actually *have* to spend. You can be profitable on paper but broke in reality if your money hasn't arrived yet.

- **Operating activities** — day-to-day income and expenses
- **Investing activities** — buying or selling assets
- **Financing activities** — loans, equity, repayments

"Your bank account doesn't lie — it reflects your actual survival timeline."

Founders who know how to read and interpret these three reports are always a step ahead.

BONUS: Benchmarks and Ratios Every Founder Should Monitor

Benchmarks help you understand how your business compares to industry norms. Here are the essential ones:

- **Gross Margin (%)** = (Revenue - Cost of Goods Sold) / Revenue
- **Net Profit Margin (%)** = Net Profit / Revenue
- **Current Ratio** = Current Assets / Current Liabilities (should be >1.2)

- **Quick Ratio** = (Cash + Receivables) / Current Liabilities
- **Burn Rate** = Monthly cash outflow (used in forecasting runway)
- **Break-even Point** = Fixed Costs / (Price per Unit – Variable Cost per Unit)

Helpful Insight: Investors often look for consistent growth in gross margin and a burn rate that suggests you can reach the next milestone before you need more funding.

Resource Tip: Crunchbase, PitchBook, and industry association reports often provide useful sector-specific benchmarks.

BONUS: What Investors Look For in Your Financials

Investors care about numbers because numbers predict behavior:

They ask:

- Can you return 10x on my investment?
- Do you understand your own metrics?
- Can you responsibly scale?

Their favorite indicators:

- Monthly Recurring Revenue (MRR)

- Customer Acquisition Cost (CAC)
- Customer Lifetime Value (LTV)
- Payback Period
- Revenue Growth Rate

Founder's Tip: Create an "Investor Snapshot" sheet that summarizes your top 10 financial KPIs on one page. It shows you're organized, proactive, and focused.

BONUS: Founder's Daily Financial Pulse

Don't just outsource your numbers — own them.

A 15-minute daily ritual:

1. Open your business bank account app
2. Check your cash balance
3. Review incoming payments and follow up
4. Compare yesterday's revenue to forecast
5. Scan for any abnormal expenses

Doing this consistently:

- Builds discipline
- Reduces money anxiety
- Catches problems early

Recommended Tool: Relay Bank for cash flow dashboards, and QuickBooks for transaction-level clarity.

(Other content remains as previously expanded: Global Insights, VC vs Bootstrapping Lens, Finance Templates, Final Word on Finance.)

6

BUILDING A LEGAL AND COMPLIANCE FRAMEWORK

"A business without legal structure is like a house without a foundation — it may look good today, but it can collapse at the first storm."

Every founder dreams of a business that grows. But sustainable growth doesn't happen without structure. It's not enough to have a good product — you need the right legal footing, protections, and responsibilities in place.

In this section, we'll walk through your essential legal toolkit: what entity to choose, what documents to create, how to handle compliance, and how to protect your intellectual property from day one.

Highly searched keywords: LLC vs S Corp, startup legal checklist, small business licenses, intellectual property protection, EIN vs ITIN, startup compliance guide, legal structure for startup, how to register a business, business formation steps, startup legal mistakes

Choosing the Right Legal Entity

Your legal structure affects everything from taxes to liability to fundraising. Choosing incorrectly can lead to tax headaches, legal exposure, or trouble attracting investors.

Common Options:

- **Sole Proprietorship**: Easiest and cheapest to form, but offers no liability protection. Best for freelancers or solopreneurs testing a concept.
- **LLC (Limited Liability Company)**: Most popular for early-stage startups. Combines liability protection with operational flexibility. Can elect to be taxed as a pass-through or corporation.
- **S Corporation**: Offers pass-through taxation and the ability to avoid self-employment tax on some earnings. Must pay owner a reasonable salary.
- **C Corporation**: Preferred by VCs and institutional investors. Allows for easier equity distribution, multiple stock classes, and stock-based compensation plans.

"Choose your structure based not just on where you are today, but where you want to go."

Historical Insight: Many legendary companies — Apple, Google, Amazon — began as C-Corps. Their ability to issue shares and scale quickly was central to their success.

Global Note:

In the UK: Consider LTD (Private Limited Company). In Canada: Corporations offer similar liability and tax benefits. In India: Private Limited Companies (Pvt Ltd) are common startup structures.

Founder's Tip: If you're building something that could attract institutional capital, go with a Delaware C-Corp from day one. Investors know and trust it. Legal credibility builds investor trust.

Required Documents for Startup Formation

Each jurisdiction may vary slightly, but foundational legal documents include:

- **Articles of Incorporation (or Organization)**: Filed with your Secretary of State. Establishes your company legally.
- **EIN (Employer Identification Number)**: Your business's tax ID. Required for banking, hiring, and tax filings. (Apply for free via the IRS website.)
- **Operating Agreement (for LLCs) or Bylaws (for Corporations)**: Describes how the business will be governed, who owns what, voting procedures, profit sharing, etc.

- **Founders Agreement**: Covers equity splits, vesting schedules, roles, and what happens if someone leaves.
- **Business Licenses & Permits**: Depends on your industry and city. Check with your local county clerk or city hall.
- **Trademark Application**: Use the USPTO.gov database to confirm brand availability.

"An operating agreement is like a prenuptial for co-founders — write it when times are good, to protect when things get tough."

BONUS RESOURCE: See Appendix for:

- Editable Operating Agreement Template
- EIN application walkthrough
- Sample Founders Agreement
- Secretary of State links by U.S. state

Real-World Advice: Don't download legal documents from a random internet search. Use state-specific forms or partner with a business formation service.

Compliance Isn't Glamorous — But It's Required

The best way to avoid regulatory problems is to start organized. Put annual compliance on your calendar and automate where possible.

Annual/Quarterly Compliance Checklist:

- **Annual Report** to your Secretary of State
- **Franchise Taxes** (even if no income was earned)
- **Registered Agent Info** must remain current
- **State and Local Permits** must be renewed
- **Sales Tax Registration** where applicable (use tools like TaxJar or Avalara)
- **1099s and W-2s**: Required for contractors and employees
- **Data Protection Policies**: If handling customer info, comply with GDPR, CCPA, etc.

"Treat compliance as part of your brand. Trust is built through diligence."

Helpful Tools:

- **Clerky** – Legal docs for startups
- **Stripe Atlas** – Incorporate & open bank accounts globally
- **ZenBusiness** – Full formation and compliance service
- **Northwest Registered Agent** – Annual filings, agent services
- **LegalZoom** – Accessible option for small businesses
- **Harbor Compliance** – Best for highly regulated industries

Founder Practice: Keep a shared compliance calendar (Google or Asana) and assign someone to audit your obligations quarterly.

Protecting Intellectual Property (IP)

Ideas are currency — protect yours early.

Types of IP:

- **Trademarks**: Names, logos, slogans. Apply via USPTO.gov or international equivalents (WIPO).
- **Copyrights**: Written works, video, audio, code. Automatically yours upon creation, but registration adds legal strength.
- **Patents**: Unique inventions, designs, or processes. Apply via USPTO. Use a patent attorney if possible.
- **Trade Secrets**: Proprietary methods, customer lists, formulas — protected by confidentiality, not registration.

Best Practices:

- Use NDAs with partners, freelancers, and early hires.
- Register trademarks in top export countries if going global.
- If using contractors, clarify IP ownership transfers in writing.
- Keep detailed version logs and timestamps of original content.

"The difference between a brand and a hustle is legal protection."

Cautionary Tale:

A small business in LA launched a skincare brand without checking trademarks. A year later, a national brand sued them and forced a rebrand — costing $30,000+. Always check name availability before investing in packaging, design, or marketing.

Founder Reflection Prompt: What is the most valuable original creation in your business — and how are you protecting it?

BONUS: Red Flags That Scare Investors and Partners

Before any funding round or acquisition, due diligence begins. Common problems include:

- No formal founder agreement or equity vesting
- Missing corporate records or filings
- Unpaid taxes or lack of compliance history
- Lawsuits or labor complaints
- Unprotected IP or brand confusion
- Commingled personal and business accounts
- No clear data privacy policy (for SaaS or D2C startups)

"If you can't get through legal due diligence, you won't get through the door."

How to Prepare:

- Maintain a secure folder with all key legal docs (Dropbox, Google Drive)
- Keep a clean cap table (use Carta or Pulley)
- Use version-controlled templates for all contracts
- Hire an accountant who understands startups
- Review your legal status quarterly with counsel

Global Note: In the EU, GDPR noncompliance can result in fines over €20M. If you collect user data, even with a simple newsletter — make sure you comply.

Final Word on Legal Structure

The most successful founders aren't just visionary — they're compliant. Legal protection helps you scale, hire, raise funds, and sleep soundly.

"Don't build your empire on sand. Lay your legal bricks early."

Founder Action Prompt: Schedule a legal audit for your business within the next 7 days. Use the checklist provided in the Appendix.

7

MARKETING AND MESSAGING FOR MAXIMUM IMPACT

"Marketing is no longer about the stuff you make but about the stories you tell." — *Seth Godin*

Marketing isn't just advertising. It's about understanding people, communicating value, and helping them say "yes" to you over anyone else. In today's fast-moving, multi-channel world, building your message and market strategy is one of the most important early investments you can make.

This section will teach you how to find your voice, identify your audience, and speak to them in a way that feels authentic, engaging, and impossible to ignore. Marketing is emotional — and as a new founder, your fresh passion can be your biggest asset if you communicated right.

Highly searched keywords: startup marketing strategy, branding for small business, best social media platforms for startups, how to create a marketing plan, storytelling for business, startup customer acquisition, how to find your niche, personal brand building

Defining Your Message: What You Say and How You Say It

Start With the Five W's:

You heard me in the video — this is your compass:

- **Who** are you serving? Get specific. Not "everyone." What age? Income? Struggle?
- **What** is your product/service and how does it fix their problem?
- **When** will they use it or need it? Timing affects demand and pricing.
- **Where** do they shop, scroll, and spend? That's where *you* must be.
- **Why** would they choose *you*? Not your category — *you*.

These questions sound simple, but most founders don't answer them well. Pause here. Answer them on paper. It will sharpen everything that follows.

> *"If you confuse, you lose. If you clarify, you convert."* — Donald Miller

Historical Insight:

Apple's 1984 ad didn't sell a computer. It sold rebellion, liberation, and the idea that Apple users *thought differently*. Your product is the tool — your message is the movement.

Messaging Checklist:

- Write a 1-sentence value proposition: "We help [X] achieve [Y] by doing [Z]."
- Create a customer-facing mission statement (try it without corporate speak)
- Use mirroring: speak like your customer speaks
- A/B test email subject lines, social captions, and video intros — data reveals clarity

Pro Tip: Use Pollfish, Wynter, or even IG Stories polls to validate messaging with real people.

Building a Memorable Brand

A brand is not a logo. It's not a font. It's what people *say* about you when you're not in the room.

Brand is Memory + Emotion

Ask yourself:

- What emotion do I want to be remembered for?
- What does my brand *feel* like?

Foundational Elements:

- **Name** (unique, searchable, trademark-safe)
- **Logo & Colors** (evoke emotion — not just aesthetics)
- **Voice** (Formal? Youthful? Bold? Quiet?)
- **Imagery** (consistent photo style, iconography, filters)

Examples:

- **Nike**: They don't just sell shoes — they inspire victory.
- **Patagonia**: Their mission to "save the planet" is louder than any product page.
- **Glossier**: They gave everyday women the mic in beauty. That's branding.

"A brand is a set of expectations, memories, stories, and relationships." — Seth Godin

Free Tools: Canva Brand Kit, Looka (logos), Coolors (color palettes)

Crafting Your Go-to-Market (GTM) Strategy

What It Is:

GTM isn't just launch day. It's your *game plan* for how you'll:

- Reach your customers
- Convert them into buyers
- Keep them coming back

Components:

- **Target Persona** (based on 5Ws)
- **Messaging Matrix** (tailored language by channel)
- **Sales Path**: How will they buy? What's your conversion journey?
- **Content Strategy**: What stories will you tell?
- **Distribution Channels**: Where will you post, sell, speak, share?

Historical Example:

Dropbox launched with a simple explainer video — and grew 70,000 waitlist signups *overnight*. No paid ads. Just story + clarity + a CTA.

Channel Guide:

Funnel Stage	Channel	Tool
Awareness	Instagram, TikTok, PR	Metricool, Brand24
Education	YouTube, Podcasts	Riverside.fm, Notion
Conversion	Shopify, Webinars	Kajabi, Typeform
Retention	Email, SMS, Community	Klaviyo, Discord

Storytelling as a Strategic Advantage

Humans are wired for narrative. Stories engage more brain activity than facts. In business, story beats specs every time.

Great Story Frameworks:

- **The Hero's Journey**: Your customer is Luke Skywalker. You're Yoda.
- **Before/After/Bridge**: "Here's the problem, here's the dream, here's how we get there."
- **PAS (Problem, Agitate, Solve)**: Spotlight the pain. Make it sting. Then offer relief.

"Stories are data with a soul." — *Brené Brown*

Founder Exercise:

Write your story *from the customer's eyes*. "I was frustrated with ____ until I found ____." This creates empathy and memorability.

Measuring What Matters

Don't just *do* marketing — measure it.

Track:

- Cost per Lead (CPL)
- Email Open Rate
- LTV:CAC Ratio (Customer Lifetime Value vs. Acquisition Cost)
- Churn rate (especially for subscriptions)

Use these numbers to guide:

- Budget decisions
- Messaging pivots
- Product improvements

Free Tools: Google Analytics, Hotjar, HubSpot CRM (free tier), Bitly for tracking links

Final Word on Marketing

In the lecture, I told you: "Marketing is your love letter to the customer." That's not fluff — that's how you build loyalty.

Don't market like a machine. Be human. Be clear. Be consistent. Let your product solve something real, and let your voice reflect the *why* behind it.

"Your brand is the single most important investment you can make in your business." — *Steve Forbes*

Founder Action Prompt: Schedule 1 hour this week to map your full customer journey — from first scroll to first purchase to repeat loyalty.

8

Building Your Operational Backbone

"Vision without execution is hallucination." — Thomas Edison

Many entrepreneurs can dream. Fewer can deliver. Operations are the engine that makes your idea move. And if you're truly trying to scale, structure and systems aren't optional — they're critical.

This section breaks down how to build operations that support growth, adapt to change, and deliver excellence day after day.

Highly searched keywords: startup operations plan, systems and processes for small business, how to scale a startup, SOP templates, startup automation tools, operational efficiency for entrepreneurs

What Are Operations, Really?

Operations are how your business gets done:

- How orders are fulfilled
- How services are delivered
- How quality is maintained
- How people are hired, managed, and evaluated

Key Areas of Startup Operations:

- **Fulfillment/Delivery**: Logistics, inventory, shipping, packaging, onboarding
- **Customer Support**: Ticketing, response time, resolution workflows
- **Human Resources**: Hiring, onboarding, payroll, training, benefits
- **Internal Processes**: SOPs (Standard Operating Procedures), internal documentation, workflows

"Build systems, not silos."

Founder Reflection: "In my early days, I mistook hustle for systems. Once I built even a basic checklist and trained one assistant, I realized scale doesn't come from doing more — it comes from structuring better."

Systems Thinking for Founders

Great founders think in systems:

- What are the repeatable steps in your business?
- How can you automate or delegate those steps?
- What happens if *you* are not around?

Tools for Systemization:

- **ClickUp / Asana / Notion** – Task management, SOP tracking

- **Zapier / Make** – Connect tools and automate workflows
- **Slack + Google Workspace** – Team collaboration, documentation

Exercise: Document one critical process (e.g., onboarding a new client). Use bullet steps. Share it with a team member. Ask them to follow it. Refine.

> *Quote from Lecture: "Too many founders are the only ones who know how anything works. That's not ownership — that's operational insecurity. Document. Teach. Replace yourself in key tasks."*

Historical Example:

McDonald's didn't grow because of burgers — they scaled because of Ray Kroc's relentless dedication to process replication. Every fryer, register, and employee had a manual. That's systems thinking at scale.

SOPs: Your Secret Weapon

Standard Operating Procedures (SOPs) help you scale. They:

- Improve quality and consistency
- Reduce mistakes
- Make onboarding easier
- Prepare you for growth or sale

What to SOP:

- Sales call scripts
- Customer onboarding checklists
- Monthly bookkeeping workflow
- Employee onboarding packet

"The business that documents, wins."

Free Resource: See Appendix for SOP Template

Founder Wisdom: "Even if you're the only employee today, write your SOPs. They are your future team's roadmap and your investor's proof that you take operations seriously."

Hiring and Team Building

Hiring your first (or next) employee is a leap. Do it intentionally.

Key Questions:

- What problem will they solve?
- Do you need full-time, part-time, or contractor?
- What's the culture you want to build?

Early-Stage Hiring Priorities:

1. Virtual Assistant / Admin Support
2. Customer Success or Operations
3. Marketing or Sales Support

Pro Tip: Use a scorecard during interviews. Rate each candidate on 3–5 traits that matter most.

Startup Insight: Netflix's early hiring philosophy was "hire adults." That meant finding people who self-manage, improve systems, and don't need babysitting. As a founder, that's golden.

Data and Operational KPIs

You can't improve what you don't measure. Choose KPIs (Key Performance Indicators) that reflect *your* growth stage.

Example KPIs by Department:

- **Customer Service**: First response time, resolution rate
- **Fulfillment**: On-time delivery rate, return rate
- **HR**: Employee retention, time to hire
- **Finance**: Expense variance, payroll accuracy

"What gets measured gets managed." — Peter Drucker

Founder Action Prompt: Choose 3 KPIs and track them weekly for 30 days.

Mentorship Note:

Too many founders track *vanity metrics* — like social followers — but not whether they're delivering great service or shipping on time. Metrics must connect to mission.

Crisis and Contingency Planning

COVID-19 proved it: every business needs a plan B. Ask yourself:

- What happens if your top vendor shuts down?
- What if your website goes offline?
- How do you communicate during crisis?

Crisis Playbook Essentials:

- Emergency contact list
- Cloud backup of critical files
- Public response protocol
- Key service-level agreements (SLAs)

"Hope is not a strategy. Resilience is."

Pro Tip: Do a "tabletop drill" — simulate a crisis and test your response.

Historical Comparison: In 2008, Airbnb founders turned crisis into creativity. With funding tight, they sold Obama-themed cereal boxes during the U.S. election. Their scrappiness bought them time to iterate. That's operational resilience.

Final Word on Operations

Startups that scale aren't just lucky. They're intentional. They invest early in building operational clarity. The more your back-end is optimized, the more your front-end can grow.

"Startups don't die from lack of ideas. They die from lack of execution." — Ben Horowitz

Founder Action Prompt: Choose one workflow this week and build a simple SOP for it. It's your first step toward operational freedom.

Final Thought from Video: "Don't chase the flash. Chase the function. Your reputation is in the repeatability of your service."

9

The People — Leadership, Advisors, and Building Culture

"You don't build a business. You build people, and people build the business." — Zig Ziglar

Your product matters. Your numbers matter. But it's your people — and the culture you build around them — that determine how far your company will go.

In this section, we'll unpack what it means to be a leader, how to find and work with advisors, and how to build a strong culture from the ground up — especially when you're starting with a small team and big dreams.

Highly searched keywords: startup leadership development, building company culture, how to find a mentor, startup advisory board, team dynamics for entrepreneurs, emotional intelligence in business

Leadership Begins with You

Leadership isn't about hierarchy — it's about *responsibility*. You set the tone for your business, especially in its earliest stages. Culture isn't written — it's *modeled*.

> *Founder Note: "I've learned the hard way — your team won't be more disciplined, communicative, or visionary than you are. You teach behavior by example, whether you mean to or not."*

Founder's Self-Check:

- Are you clear on your personal leadership values?
- Do you respond to pressure with principle?
- Can you articulate your company's mission in 30 seconds?
- Are you investing time to grow as a communicator?
- Do you schedule regular 1-on-1s to stay connected to your team?

> *"People don't leave jobs — they leave managers."*

Quote from Lecture:

> *"I told you all, this isn't just about profits — this is about posture. How you stand up when things go wrong, how you speak when things get tense — your leadership shows most in silence and stress."*

Deep Dive:

Effective leadership includes managing energy, not just time. Founders who build morning routines, protect focused work time, and create clear expectations are respected. Create a vision document — a single-page outline of who you want to be as a leader, how you'll grow, and how you'll serve your team.

"Clarity is kindness." — Brené Brown

The Power of Advisors and Mentors

You can't see your blind spots. That's where advisors come in. The best founders surround themselves with experienced voices who challenge and guide them.

Where to Find Advisors:

- Startup accelerators (Y Combinator, Techstars, Founder Institute)
- LinkedIn (mutual connections, alumni networks)
- Founder communities (Indie Hackers, MicroConf, On Deck)
- Alumni from past jobs or universities

Pro Tip: Instead of asking someone to "be your mentor," try asking: "Could I get 15 minutes of your time to ask one or two questions about [specific topic]?" Then follow up with gratitude and share results. That's how relationships begin.

Building an Advisory Board:

- Choose 2–4 advisors with complementary strengths (e.g., legal, product, marketing, finance)
- Set expectations: frequency of meetings, form of communication
- Offer small equity stakes (0.25%–1% common stock) for meaningful contributors
- Use a quarterly email update to keep advisors engaged and aligned

Historical Example: Jeff Bezos kept an informal braintrust early on — executives from retail, tech, and logistics. These minds helped him shape Amazon before it was a juggernaut.

Bonus Insight:

Build a "wisdom cabinet" — a small list of 3–5 trusted voices you can turn to. You don't need everyone to agree. You need different angles to see clearly.

Quote: "Smart founders talk to people who have seen tomorrow."

Hiring with Heart and Strategy

Hiring isn't about filling seats — it's about amplifying your mission. The first 5–10 hires at a startup shape everything: speed, quality, resilience, and even future culture.

Traits to Look for in Early Hires:

- Grit: Do they follow through?
- Curiosity: Do they ask great questions?
- Integrity: Do they take ownership for mistakes?
- Coachability: Can they grow and adapt?

Red Flags:

- "That's not my job" attitude
- No examples of past ownership or accountability
- Poor communication skills
- Short attention spans across roles or companies

"Hire for attitude. Train for skill."

Founder Reflection:

"I used to hire based on résumés. Now I hire based on character. Because when you're building something from scratch, people's values will shape every decision."

Best Practice:

Involve your existing team in hiring. A short 'test project' can reveal more than three interviews. Debrief with your team. Culture is everyone's responsibility.

Building a Culture That Scales

Culture isn't ping-pong tables and swag — it's *how* work gets done. It's the habits, rituals, and unspoken rules that drive decision-making.

Keys to Great Culture:

- Psychological safety — can your team speak up?
- Clear values — what behaviors are celebrated?
- Shared rituals — do you celebrate wins?
- Accountability with grace — how are mistakes handled?

Case Study: Netflix

Netflix's "Culture Deck" changed the startup world. They prioritized freedom and responsibility, embraced radical candor, and documented expectations openly. The result? A high-performing, high-trust workplace that attracted elite talent.

Founder Insight:

Define your values while your team is still small. Make them visible — on walls, in Slack channels, in team check-ins. And live them as the founder.

Exercise: Write a one-page "culture vision" — what do you want your team to say about your company after their first year?

Mini Exercise: Ask your team anonymously what three words describe your company's culture today — and what three they'd *like* it to be. Review results, and adjust.

Emotional Intelligence (EQ) in Leadership

EQ isn't soft — it's *strategic*. It helps you:

- Navigate conflict
- Motivate your team
- Adapt to change

Components of EQ:

- Self-awareness
- Empathy
- Active listening
- Constructive feedback

"IQ gets you hired. EQ gets you promoted." — Daniel Goleman

From the Video:

"Y'all hear me — don't just work on the business. Work on *you*. The business will only go as far as your healing, your maturity, and your awareness."

Expansion:

EQ in leadership includes being able to:

- De-escalate tension quickly
- Read energy shifts on your team
- Hold tough performance conversations with compassion
- Apologize sincerely when you miss the mark

Founder Tip: Make feedback a habit. Ask regularly: "What's one thing I could do better as a founder this week?" And actually listen.

Final Word on People and Culture

You can't scale without people. And people won't stay — or thrive — without intentional leadership, honest feedback, and authentic culture.

Be the leader you needed when you started. Teach what you've learned. Model what you expect.

Founder Action Prompt: Write a letter to your future team — what do you hope they believe about your leadership five years from now?

Bonus Action: Create a "Team Welcome Guide" — one simple PDF with your values, work style, communication expectations, and how to thrive together.

> *"Leadership is not about being in charge. It's about taking care of those in your charge." — Simon Sinek*

10

Launching, Growing, and Pivoting with Purpose

"In preparing for battle I have always found that plans are useless, but planning is indispensable." — Dwight D. Eisenhower

This section is your roadmap to executing what you've built. From the first launch to the scaling years, and even the moments you need to pivot — this is where theory becomes traction. Launching a startup is not simply the culmination of preparation; it is a test of your ability to adapt, listen, respond, and lead in real time. Be prepared to experiment, fail fast, and remain open to feedback from your users, your data, and your instincts.

Highly searched keywords: startup launch strategy, product-market fit, go-to-market (GTM), growth hacking techniques, startup KPIs, pivot vs persevere, startup launch checklist, lean startup launch, iterative product development, customer feedback loop, founder journaling, pre-launch campaigns

1. Launching: Readiness Meets Opportunity

Launching your product or service is more than an event — it's a *series of deliberate decisions* backed by insight, preparedness, and relationship-building. Think of launch not as a destination but as the beginning of an ongoing conversation with your market.

Expanded Pre-Launch Checklist:

- ☑ Minimum Viable Product (MVP) is functional, stable, and focused on core utility
- ☑ Early user feedback obtained through interviews, prototypes, A/B tests
- ☑ Website, user journey, and checkout tested across browsers and mobile
- ☑ Support infrastructure: FAQs, live chat options, ticketing system ready
- ☑ Defined marketing narrative and positioning tested with pilot group
- ☑ Metrics dashboard in place to track usage, engagement, and retention post-launch
- ☑ Email list pre-segmented for personalized outreach
- ☑ Social proof lined up: testimonials, beta case studies, or influencer validation

Encouragement: Remember, your first launch is the worst your product will ever be. Stay humble, stay accessible, and *always* invite critique.

"The best founders don't try to be perfect — they try to get better, faster." — W.M. Cornell

Soft Launch vs Hard Launch:

- **Soft Launch**: Allows feedback before scale. Often tested with a pilot group, industry insiders, or local community.
- **Hard Launch**: Requires readiness across marketing, logistics, and operations. Press coverage, events, and ad spend often accompany this stage.

Case Study: Airbnb Before scaling globally, Airbnb founders manually photographed listings, stayed with hosts, and interviewed guests. The lesson? *Start small. Learn fast.*

2. Go-To-Market Strategy (GTM)

A GTM strategy isn't a marketing plan — it's a holistic blueprint for delivering value. Think of it as the bridge between what you've built and those who need it most.

Deeper GTM Components:

- **Segmentation**: Define segments within your market — what pain points, habits, or preferences distinguish them?
- **Messaging Hierarchy**: Craft 3–5 positioning pillars that resonate emotionally and logically with your target market.
- **Channel Testing**: Use small budgets across multiple channels. Kill what doesn't work. Double down on winners.
- **Customer Journey Mapping**: Use real user behavior, not assumptions. Tools like Hotjar and FullStory can help visualize friction points.
- **Influencer Engagement**: Consider micro-influencers aligned with your niche over high-cost, low-conversion celebrities.

Exercise: Write a 150-character version of your value proposition for a Facebook ad. Then expand it to a 3-minute pitch deck opening. This gives you range and clarity.

3. Growth: Strategies for Sustainable Scaling

Sustainable growth is *measured*, *intentional*, and *user-centric*. Avoid vanity metrics. Focus on what drives long-term loyalty and referrals.

Additional Growth Techniques:

- **Lifecycle Email Marketing**: Automate email journeys for onboarding, activation, upsells, and churn prevention.
- **Community-Led Growth**: Launch a private Slack group, Discord, or Facebook group to build direct connection.
- **Content Flywheel**: Record a webinar > transcribe it > turn it into a blog > slice into social posts > create email drip. One piece = 10 assets.
- **Product-Led Growth**: Build product features that *encourage* users to invite others (think: collaboration tools, shared dashboards, or rewards).

Suggested Weekly Growth Ritual:

- Track 3 KPIs daily
- Run weekly team growth brainstorm (include marketing, product, and support)
- Celebrate one customer success story per week

"Customer delight is the most underutilized marketing channel." — *W.M. Cornell*

4. When It's Time to Pivot

You pivot when data consistently disproves your hypothesis — and curiosity remains alive. Pivoting is courageous. It's a declaration that your mission is greater than your ego.

Tools for Evaluating Pivots:

- **Five Whys Analysis**: Ask "Why?" five times about every failed outcome to get to the root.
- **Cohort Analysis**: Examine retention by signup date or segment. This reveals if newer users are faring better or worse.
- **Net Promoter Score (NPS) Comments**: Group by sentiment to see consistent themes

Encouragement: Pivot doesn't mean panic. It means progress. Be honest. Be iterative. Be clear with your stakeholders.

> *"The greatest pivot is the one that brings you closer to your mission — not away from it."* — *W.M. Cornell*

5. Building Momentum and Staying Aligned

Momentum isn't loud — it's cumulative. It comes from *alignment* across leadership, product, operations, and culture.

Expanded Weekly Rituals:

- Monday: Intention setting (1 personal, 1 team, 1 product)
- Wednesday: Learning lunch — a team member shares one insight, book, or metric
- Friday: Wins + gratitude recap

Strategic Tools:

- **Founder Journal**: Document decisions, lessons, and shifts weekly. This becomes your "Operating Bible."
- **Mural Board / Visual KPI Tracker**: Visualize your wins and bottlenecks side by side.
- **Mid-Quarter Reflection**: Don't wait for retros. Pause and realign every 6 weeks.

Founder Reminder: What gets scheduled gets done. Treat your rest and self-development like product features — they impact output.

> "If you burn out, your company burns out. Rest is resistance. Recovery is strategy." — W.M. Cornell

Closeout Action Items:

- Identify your next 12-week goal
- Schedule your next founder retreat or mental health day.

- Write a thank-you letter to a customer, teammate, or mentor

Final Thought:

This journey will stretch your skills, test your stamina, and refine your spirit. But if you lead with integrity, learn continuously, and build with intention, you will create something of lasting impact.

"Don't chase scale. Chase significance."

The best companies aren't always the first movers. They're the most thoughtful. They respond faster. They learn deeper. They serve better.

Your time is now. Let's build.

"Entrepreneurship isn't about being fearless. It's about acting in the face of fear — for something greater than yourself." — W.M. Cornell

11

Corporate Structures, Veils, and Entity Wisdom

In this section, we take a deep dive into the layered strategy of structuring your business for longevity, flexibility, and corporate protection. This is not just a legal lesson — it's a foundational shift in how you relate to ownership, identity, and wealth.

This section is a masterclass on legal architecture. It isn't just about compliance — it's about understanding the deep roots of how wealth is structured and preserved. It reflects wisdom earned through experience, failure, mentorship, and history. This is where the novice becomes the strategist.

What is a Corporation — and Why Was It Invented?

Historically, corporations were formed to support joint ventures — often seafaring missions from Europe — where investors shared profits and risks. The legal concept allowed for continuity, asset ownership, and minimized liability.

> *"A corporation is a person in the eyes of the law. It exists until it is terminated, closed, or penalized."*

The idea is longevity. Coca-Cola, McDonald's, IBM — these brands live on through legal entities that survive their founders. Your goal is the same: build something bigger than yourself.

Historical Perspective: Where Corporations Come From

In Europe's Age of Exploration, joint ventures — like the Dutch East India Company — were backed by investors who shared profits and losses. The modern corporation was born to enable shared enterprise with limited liability.

Corporations became the legal vehicles for enduring ventures, innovations, and institutions. Their longevity wasn't an accident — it was engineered.

> *"Coca-Cola still exists. Its founder does not. That's the power of the corporate veil and structure."*

The Corporate Veil and Why It Matters

The corporate veil separates the business's legal and financial obligations from your personal life. This line is your shield. It protects your assets, your credit, your name.

> *"The entire goal of forming a company is to not be personally exposed to the liabilities of that company."*

The veil can only be created and maintained through structure — not convenience.

Understanding Business Entities: Beyond Just Letters

Let's clarify the real differences between these structures:

- **LLC (Limited Liability Company)**: Offers flexible management and pass-through taxation, protective, and commonly used. Allows multiple members, has fewer compliance burdens, and enables tax choices. The most popular choice for small businesses.

- **LLP (Limited Liability Partnership)**: Typically used in professional industries such as law and accounting. Partners share liabilities and profits. Mostly used by licensed professionals — , accountants, architects. Offers protection among partners.

- **C Corporation**: This structure exists independently of its owners, making it scalable, fundable, and durable. It pays corporate taxes and distributes profits via dividends. A fully separate legal entity that files its own taxes. Most scalable option, preferred by investors and VC firms.

- **S Corporation**: A tax designation. Meant to avoid double taxation but passes all income to the owner's personal tax return. This erodes the corporate veil. Tax classification for corporations or LLCs that pass income directly to shareholders. The downside? Limited protection and restrictions on ownership.

- **Sole Proprietorship**: Easiest to form, hardest to scale safely. You and your business are legally the same. Legally inseparable from the owner. Simple but exposes the owner to full liability.

- **General Partnership**: All partners are equally liable unless otherwise stated. Good for shared ventures, risky without protection. Two or more people join forces without forming a new legal entity. Can be dangerous without proper agreements.

"I tell my students: anytime you see an 'S' — whether it's S-Corp, single-member LLC, or sole proprietor — you are signing up for exposure. No veil. No insulation."

The S-Stigma

Real Talk: Why "S" May Mean "Self-Exposure"

The "S" is a designation for "Self"; an entity usually given by the IRS or inherent nature of the initial filing.

"Anytime you see an 'S' — Sole Proprietor, Single-Member LLC, S Corp — it means no true corporate protection."

In mentoring sessions, I teach students to be wary of structures where the entity and the individual are one and the same. The goal of corporate formation is to separate the individual from the business. That separation is your corporate veil.

The "S" designations, while convenient, tend to collapse the separation between you and your business. You are the business — and that undermines protection.

S = Self = Shared Liability

The Structure: Holding, Sector, and Operating Entities

Operating LLCs (Frontline)

Each business unit (e.g., 711 Franchise LLC, Wingstop LLC) operates under its own LLC. These are disposable, nimble, and cleanly separate.

Sector Companies (Mid-Level Management)

Group operating LLCs by industry (e.g., Retail Corp, Real Estate Corp). Each sector can be a C-Corp or LLC.

Holding Company (Control Center)

Owns all sector companies. It collects profits, distributes resources, manages risk, and owns valuable assets. This is where the founder draws income or expenses — not from the day-to-day business.

"Don't go to 7-Eleven and try to collect your cut. Let that cash filter up to the Holding Company."

Trust (Legacy Guardian)

When assets are paid off or no longer in operational use, transfer them to a Trust. Trusts offer the strongest form of asset protection and estate planning.

Creating the Corporate Pyramid

Diagram: Corporate Structure Pyramid

1. **Trust** (Top-Level)
   - Owns Holding Company
   - Holds retired assets
2. **Holding Company**
   - Owns Sector Corps
   - Centralizes expenses & payroll
3. **Sector Companies** (e.g., Retail Corp, Real Estate Corp)
   - Owns Operating LLCs
4. **Operating LLCs**
   - Owns and runs individual stores
   - Contracts leases, hires staff, sells products

Operating Companies (LLCs)

Your individual business units — like your coffee shop, salon, or app company — should be legally separate LLCs. These are easy to create, flexible, and disposable if needed.

Sector Companies

Group your similar LLCs under a Sector C-Corp (e.g., Retail Corp, Real Estate Corp). This allows you to manage industries collectively and organize cash flow.

Holding Company

This is your strategic control center. All sector companies are owned by the Holding Company, which pays for shared services like your salary, your car, your housing — and benefits from centralized tax planning.

> *"The holding company is where you operate as the owner — not the operator."*

Trust

When assets are no longer in daily use — such as paid-off real estate — move them to a Trust. This ensures legacy protection and tax insulation.

Real Estate Model: The McDonald's Playbook

McDonald's corporate doesn't just sell burgers — they own the land. Every franchise location sits on property leased from corporate.

- Acquire real estate via your LLC
- When the mortgage is paid off, transfer the deed to your Trust
- Lease the property back to the business

You now own both the asset and the income stream — without co-mingling risk.

Licensing and Franchise Mechanics

"You don't own the brand — you license the right to operate under it."

Examples:

- **Verizon Kiosk at the Mall**: Authorized dealer, not Verizon corporate
- **Denny's Location**: You own the LLC; you license the brand

Each location is:

- Legally distinct
- Financially isolated
- Strategically protected

When you franchise, your real value is the agreement — not the brand. Use this understanding when creating your own licensing models.

Final Reflections: Protecting the Mission

This section is more than technical knowledge. It's a mindset shift.

> *"Structure isn't about paperwork. It's about power — and protection."*

You are not just starting a hustle. You're building a dynasty. Form that first LLC, draft your operating agreement, and set your goals on generational wealth.

Income Strategies: Beyond W-2

Most employees earn a W-2 and pay taxes on every dollar. But owners have options:

- Live off business-paid expenses (car, rent, meals)
- File a modest W-2 if needed
- Retain earnings inside the corporation (especially C Corps)
- Use depreciation to manage reported profits

Example:

A pastor owns retail coffee shops under a sector company. Rather than take a salary, the holding company pays for rent, groceries, and travel. The pastor lives well — legally and efficiently — while the entity handles the tax burden.

"When you understand the rules, you play the game differently."

Real Estate Strategy

Like McDonald's, the business (restaurant) may not be the true asset — the real estate is. Purchase properties through your LLCs, and when they are paid off, transfer them to your Trust. Then lease them back to your business.

This allows:

- Protection from operating liability
- Passive income from rent
- Asset appreciation in a legacy-friendly structure

Franchise and Licensing Models

Many franchises (like Denny's, 7-Eleven, Verizon-authorized retailers) operate this way:

- You create an LLC
- That LLC is granted a license to use the franchise's name
- You run the location under your LLC, completely separate from the parent company

This reduces risk for the brand, protects their reputation, and gives you entrepreneurial control.

"You don't own the brand — you license the right to use the name."

Compensation and Lifestyle

The game changes when your entity starts paying for your life — legally:

- Rent: Paid as corporate housing
- Transportation: Company car or mileage
- Food & entertainment: Deductible if business-related
- Clothing: If brand-marked or required

"You don't need to take a W-2 to live. You need to structure your business to take care of you."

Use tax codes, like depreciation schedules (e.g., IRS Form 4562), to reduce taxable income by amortizing purchases over time. For vehicles over 6,000 lbs (like SUVs), write-offs may reach $25K+.

Founder's Note: From Hustle to Structure

Too many founders start out hustling — working in the business instead of on it. This chapter is your wake-up call. You're not just building a job — you're building a machine. One that runs without you, protects you, and benefits you.

Start small. Form that first LLC. Open the holding company. Learn the tax code. Get a mentor. And then watch how freedom grows, not just income.

"This is how legacy is built. Structure first, scale second."

Appendix — Tools, Templates, and Resources for Founders

Welcome to your resource vault. This appendix includes real-world templates, checklists, and links to tools that can help you apply the lessons in this guide with confidence. Think of this as your toolkit for traction, troubleshooting, and transformation.

Essential Business Templates

1. Business Model Canvas

- **Purpose**: Map your key activities, value propositions, customer segments, revenue streams, and more.
- **Download**: Strategyzer Canvas Template (PDF)

2. Vision & Values Builder

- **Purpose**: Help define your company's mission, core beliefs, and leadership values.
- **Template Includes**: Vision Statement Framework, Core Values List, Founder's Manifesto Worksheet

4. Startup Budget & Financial Forecast Tool

- **Purpose**: Track your expenses, predict revenue, and manage burn rate.
- **Download**: Customized 12-month and 3-year templates for service and product-based businesses

Legal & Compliance Resources

EIN, Business License, and Incorporation Tools

- IRS EIN Online Application
- LegalZoom Business Formation Services
- Rocket Lawyer Startup Legal Templates

Operating Agreement Example

> Sample Excerpt: "ARTICLE III. MANAGEMENT The Company shall be managed by its Members. Each Member shall have full authority to act on behalf of the Company..."

Marketing & GTM Worksheets

Go-To-Market Planner

- **Includes**: Channel Selection Matrix, Messaging Pyramid, Launch Campaign Checklist

Customer Avatar Builder

- **Purpose**: Create detailed user personas
- **Tool**: HubSpot Make My Persona

Mental Resilience Toolkit

- Apps: Calm, Headspace, Stoic
- Books: "The Obstacle Is the Way" by Ryan Holiday, "Essentialism" by Greg McKeown

Accountability Partner Agreement

> Outline your shared cadence for check-ins, goals, and support boundaries.

Bonus Resources & Communities

- Indie Hackers — Community of real founders sharing lessons
- On Deck — Global founder and operator fellowships
- SCORE.org — Free mentorship for small business owners

Downloadable Resource Folder

All the above tools, templates, and sample forms are available for download at: https://www.tawcpublishing.com/business-essentials-toolbox

A Final Word of Encouragement

You are building more than a business — you are building *something only you* can create. Let this toolkit be a guide, not a crutch. The most powerful tool you'll ever use is *consistency*.

You've got this.

> *Let's build something lasting — together.*

> *— W.M. Cornell*

As with any business advice, please seek a business lawyer when it comes to legal business documentation.

Glossary of Terms

CAC (Customer Acquisition Cost) — The total cost associated with acquiring a new customer, including marketing and sales expenses.

Churn Rate — The percentage of customers who stop using your product or service over a given time period.

GTM (Go-To-Market Strategy) — A plan for how a company will deliver its product or service to customers and achieve competitive advantage.

KPI (Key Performance Indicator) — Quantifiable measurements that help a business track its progress toward goals.

LTV (Lifetime Value) — The projected revenue a customer will generate during their relationship with your business.

MVP (Minimum Viable Product) — A product with just enough features to attract early customers and validate a product idea early in the development cycle.

NPS (Net Promoter Score) — A metric that assesses customer loyalty by asking how likely customers are to recommend your product.

North Star Metric — The single metric that best captures the core value your product delivers to customers.

Pivot — A fundamental change to a startup's product, business model, or target market based on validated learning.

Retention Rate — The percentage of users who continue to use your product or service over time.

UVP (Unique Value Proposition) — A clear statement that describes the benefit of your product, how you solve your customer's needs, and what distinguishes you from the competition.

Vision Statement — A declaration of your startup's long-term goals and aspirations.

Founder Journal — A personal log maintained by a founder to track decisions, lessons learned, and strategic reflections.

Let this glossary serve as a reference to revisit when you encounter a term or need to refresh your understanding. You're not expected to know everything from the start — mastery is built, one concept at a time.

About the Author

W. M. Cornell has worked in the business finance industry for over 25 years. Her expertise in money management and reputation as a multiple business owner and consultant is unparalleled.

As the owner of Gold Leaf Alliance, a business development consulting firm, Ms. Cornell Gold Leaf Alliance, provides innovative strategies and solutions that bring success to their clients.

At a young age, Ms. Cornell could see the talent and possibilities of success in her individual family members, but lack of business knowledge and funding kept them from reaching their ultimate potential.

She made it her goal to help bridge the gap between people's innovative ideas and talent, and realizing success by helping them receive business knowledge and, ultimately, funding.

Ms. Cornell has shared what she has learned and the connections she has made in the business industry in this highly organized book as a way to extend her ability to assist entrepreneurs and those new to the business industry.

www.ingramcontent.com/pod-product-compliance
Lightning Source LLC
Chambersburg PA
CBHW030531210326
41597CB00014B/1113